This Black Coloring Book
Belongs to

Welcome to my Krazy Kolorz world!

I'm so excited that you're here and ready to unleash your creativity. Whether you're an experienced artist or a beginner, you will enjoy discovering this Krazy world. I'm sure to spark your imagination and bring out the artist in you.

Inside these pages, you'll find a diverse range of illustrations that are just waiting to be brought to life with your favorite colors. From intricate patterns to a diverse range of animals, flowers, landscapes and more... there's something for everyone in this book.

So grab your markers, crayons, or colored pencils, and let's get coloring!

Happy Koloring!

Lily May Kolorz

@LILYMAYKOLORZ

Follow Me!

Visit my online store:
www.lilymaykolorz.store

FREE STUFF . SPIRAL BOUND . PRINTABLES ...

♡ 16 free printable pages to download
♡ New freebies each month
♡ Links to spiral bound books

Thanks for your trust, I am very grateful that you have chosen one of my books.

Please share your experience and coloring on Amazon and social media

TEST your kolorz

TEST your kolorz

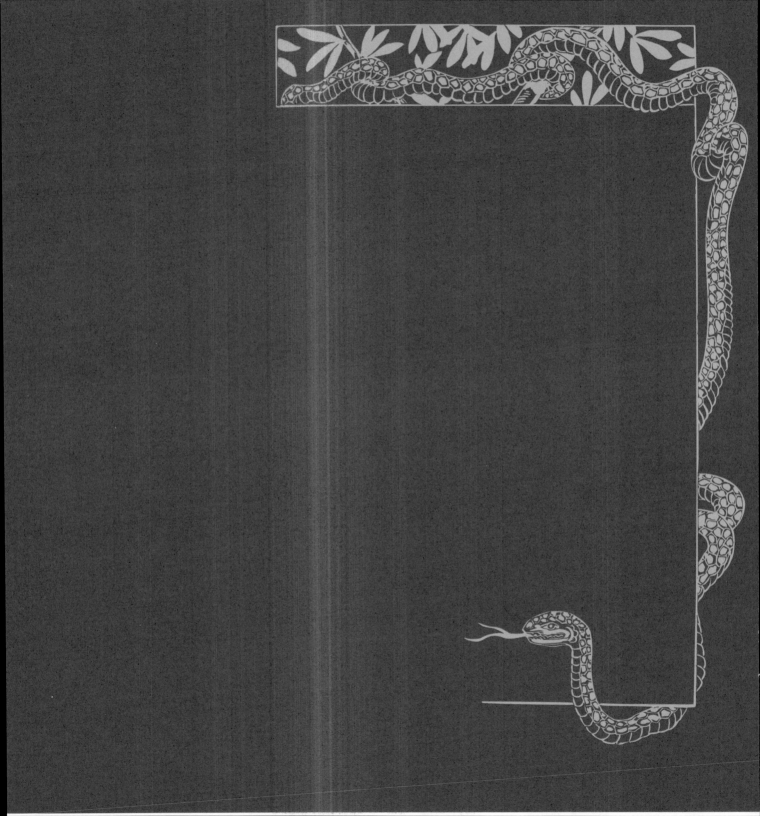

Color me BLACK

Lily May Kolorz Black Coloring Book

Fantasy Kreatures

Lily May Kolorz KAWAII COLORING BOOK

Check out other titles

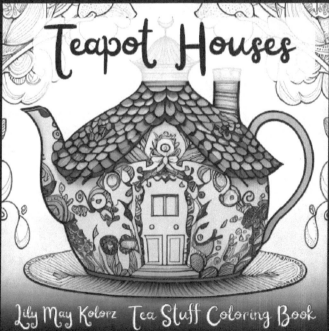

Teapot Houses

Lily May Kolorz Tea Stuff Coloring Book

Creepy Kawaii Sea Kreatures

Lily May Kolorz GRAYSCALE COLORING BOOK

WARNING:

This book is printed by Amazon so i can't control the quality.
If you have any printing quality issue claim for exchange or refund.

This book is also available in premium black ink printing with spiral bound (link on my website)

Made in United States
Troutdale, OR
07/02/2024

20955277R00040